HAKEEM OLAJUWON

Superstar Center

BY BILL GUTMAN

MILLBROOK SPORTS WORLD
THE MILLBROOK PRESS
BROOKFIELD, CONNECTICUT

Photographs courtesy of Allsport: cover (Jim Gund), cover inset (Tim DeFrisco), p. 46 (David Leah); NBA Photos: pp. 1 (Bill Baptist), 29 (Andrew D. Bernstein), 32 (Bill Baptist), 40-41 (Andrew D. Bernstein); AP/Wide World: pp. 4, 10, 16, 23, 35, 36-37, 39; Jerry Cooke/Photo Researchers: p.7; University of Houston: pp. 13, 14, 19; UPI/Bettmann: pp. 21, 25, 27; Focus on Sports: pp. 30, 44; *The Houston Post*: p. 42.

Library of Congress Cataloging-in-Publication Data
Hakeem Olajuwon, superstar center / by Bill Gutman
p. cm. —(Millbrook sports world)
Includes bibliographical references (p.).
ISBN 1-56294-568-8
Summary: A biography of basketball star center Hakeem Olajuwon, from his childhood in Nigeria to his early success at the University of Houston to his star status with the Houston Rockets as the first player in history to be named NBA regular-season MVP, NBA finals MVP, and Defensive Player of the Year in the same season (1994).

1. Olajuwon, Hakeem, 1963–   —Juvenile literature. 2. Basketball players—United States—Biography—Juvenile literature. 3. National Basketball Association—Juvenile literature. [1. Olajuwon, Hakeem, 1963– . 2. Basketball players. 3. Blacks—Nigeria—Biography.] I. Title. II. Series.
GV884.043G88 1995 796.323′092—dc20 [B] 94-48158 CIP AC
Published by The Millbrook Press, Inc.
2 Old New Milford Road
Brookfield, Connecticut 06804

HAKEEM
OLAJUWON

It was the sixth game of the 1993–1994 National Basketball Association (NBA) championship. The Houston Rockets were facing the New York Knicks. The Knicks had a 3-2 lead in the series. If they won game six, they would be the champions. The Rockets had their backs against the wall.

With less than a minute left, the Rockets held a slim, 84–82 lead. New York had the ball, and guard John Starks tried to get it inside to the Knicks' star center, 7-foot (213-centimeter) Patrick Ewing. Quick as a flash, the Houston center darted between Starks and Ewing and stole the pass. The Knicks fouled him immediately.

With the pressure on, Hakeem Olajuwon calmly sank both free throws to give his team an 86–82 lead with just 39.3 seconds left. But the Knicks wouldn't quit. An Anthony Mason jump shot with 32 seconds remaining cut the Houston lead to 86-84. When the Rockets missed a shot with just 8 seconds left, New York got the rebound and had a chance to tie or win it.

Hakeem's heroics allowed the Houston Rockets to win the sixth game of the 1993–1994 NBA finals and send the series to a seventh and deciding game. Here Hakeem drives around Knicks star Patrick Ewing en route to a 30-point performance.

As the clock ticked down, the Knicks looked for a final shot. The ball went to Starks behind the three-point line on the left side of the basket. With time almost gone, Starks launched a jump shot. If it went in, the Knicks would win the game and the championship.

But just as Starks released the ball, the outstretched hand of Hakeem Olajuwon seemed to come out of nowhere. The Rockets center had quickly come away from guarding Ewing to challenge the shot. He leaped as high as his 7-foot (213-centimeter) frame would take him and just barely ticked the ball as it came off Starks's hand.

It was just enough of a deflection to send the ball off its mark. The buzzer sounded as the shot missed. All the Rockets and the fans who packed the Summit Arena in Houston breathed a sigh of relief. Their team had won the game, 86-84, thanks to the inspired play of Hakeem Olajuwon. The man who had been the NBA's Most Valuable Player during the regular season had rescued his team again.

Hakeem had scored 30 points and grabbed 10 rebounds in that crucial sixth game. But his block of Starks's 3-point try was perhaps the biggest play of his life. He had ensured his team a seventh and deciding game for the championship. And a championship was the one thing that Hakeem Olajuwon had not won.

Now it was there for the taking.

A DIFFERENT KIND OF CHILDHOOD

Hakeem Abdul Olajuwon did not follow the usual road to basketball stardom. When Hakeem came to the NBA in 1984, he had been playing basketball for fewer than six years and had been considered a star for only two. The reason for his late start was simple. Hakeem had grown up in Africa, where basketball was not an important sport. In fact, he didn't play the sport at all until he was 15 years old.

Hakeem was born in Lagos, the largest city in the African country of Nigeria, on January 21, 1963. There were nearly six million people in Lagos then. The city was like many large cities in the United States. There were many poor people and many people without jobs.

The Olajuwon family was better off than many others. Hakeem's parents, Salaam and Abike, had their own cement business. It didn't make them rich, but gave them enough to support their six children. They all lived in a one-story, three-bedroom house behind a small, fenced courtyard. As followers of the Islamic religion, Hakeem, his four brothers, and his sister were raised as Muslims, and the whole family prayed daily.

As a youngster, Hakeem was very shy. He usually went out of his way to avoid trouble of any kind. He spent his time playing soccer and handball.

Hakeem especially excelled at handball. The game in Nigeria wasn't the same as handball in the United States, where players

A crowded street in Lagos, Nigeria, the city where Hakeem was born. Many of the people in Lagos are poor and have had to struggle all their lives.

hit a small rubber ball up against a high wall. In Lagos, handball was played by passing a ball up and down a field and trying to score by throwing it into a shortened soccer net.

"Every time I touch the ball, I score," Hakeem once said of his handball skills.

As he got older he began to work very hard in school. His parents always told their children that they wanted them to have a good education so they could live a better life in Nigeria. They even thought about sending them to college in the United States.

Besides studying hard, Hakeem was growing quite rapidly. His father was 6 feet 3 inches (191 centimeters) tall, while his mother was also tall at 6 feet (183 centimeters). Hakeem, however, was soon taller then everyone else in the family. By the time he was 15, he was already 6 feet 9 (206 centimeters). But he was also very thin, weighing just 170 pounds (77 kilograms). By that time, he was outstanding at both soccer and handball.

Even in a country where there was very little basketball, a 15-year-old that tall is going to attract attention. Sure enough, one of the few basketball coaches in Lagos, a man named Ganiyu Otenigbagbe, found out about Hakeem and went to see him. He was the one who suggested Hakeem try a new sport. The year was 1978, and the new sport would soon change Hakeem's life.

THE ROAD TO HOUSTON

At first, basketball was not a good experience for Hakeem. Putting a ball through a metal hoop may seem easy, especially for an incredibly tall kid. But for a 15-year-old who had never played before, basketball was a tangle of arms and legs.

"I couldn't dunk then," Hakeem said. "And I couldn't lay it up, either. I didn't know how to use the backboard. So I would just try to push the ball in."

In one of the first games Hakeem played, the outcome was in doubt until the final seconds. Sure enough, he got the ball in close. Hakeem tried to push it in. The ball rolled around the rim . . . and out.

"I was so mad," he recalled. "I didn't even go back on defense. We lost the game. I remember thinking at the time, 'I give up. I don't want to play this game anymore.'"

But he didn't give up. During the next year, Hakeem slowly learned the fundamentals. Then, in 1979, he began playing with the Lagos State Juniors. They were a club team that played on an asphalt court at Rowe Park. The backboards were tilted and the rims bent. The games could be rough.

"I'd fall all the time," Hakeem said, "but I was never hurt, even though we played on concrete."

When the Juniors played at the national all-sports festival, Hakeem competed in both handball and basketball. He was the leading scorer in handball and top rebounder in basketball. Lagos State won gold medals in both. Before long, he was promoted to the Nigerian national team.

By 1980, Hakeem was attending high school but playing basketball mostly with the national team. He was their center that year and went with them to the All-African games, held in Morocco. Hakeem was one of the better players on the team, and they won a bronze medal for third place.

His parents were thinking only of his education when they suggested he go to college in the United States. Language would not be a problem. English was the primary language in Nigeria, and Hakeem spoke it with a soft British accent. But he also spoke French, as well as a total of four native Nigerian dialects.

He planned to study business in the United States. His parents felt that would best prepare him to succeed in Nigeria when he returned. An American coach in Africa, Chris Pond, suggested that Hakeem look at the University of Houston.

Hakeem started out to visit seven universities. But as soon as he arrived at the Houston campus, in October 1980, he decided to stay. Basketball coach Guy Lewis took one look at the big kid from Lagos and knew two things immediately. The first was that Hakeem had a great deal of natural talent. The second was that he was very weak in all the fundamentals of the game. Now the question was, Could he learn fast enough to help the Houston program?

It was apparent that Hakeem was not ready to play basketball for the Houston Cougars in the 1980–1981 season. So the decision was made to "red-shirt" Hakeem his freshman year. That meant he couldn't even practice with the team. But he would be able to play four full years after that.

During his first year at the University of Houston, Hakeem was not a very good basketball player. Sometimes at practice he looked more like a soccer player, bouncing the ball in the air with his foot.

Once he knew what being red-shirted meant, Hakeem vowed to learn to play the game better. "When I first came to Houston, I didn't know what I could do," he said. "I was just happy to be on the team. Then I had to watch the first year, but I always thought, 'I can do this.'"

FIRST-YEAR STRUGGLE

There was more for Hakeem to get used to in Houston than just the game of basketball. He was shy at first and didn't go out much. Making friends wasn't easy, although his good nature and positive outlook soon made him popular with the other students on campus.

Clyde Drexler, one of the stars on the Houston team when Hakeem arrived, remembers Hakeem in those early days. "He got unnerved when people weren't patient with him," Drexler recalled. "I think he was homesick a lot then, too. But we helped him and taught him our ways. He watched everything we did. He was like a hawk."

Hakeem admitted that it wasn't easy changing some of the old customs. "I was brought up to honor and respect older people," he said. "I bow to them out of respect. But there were people here who laughed at me when I did that. So I stopped."

Even though he stopped bowing, Hakeem always showed respect for everyone and rarely became angry. That's why people liked him so much.

Hakeem's grades at the university were good right from the beginning. It was his basketball playing that needed work. He began spending countless hours at the Fonde Recreation Center in Houston. During the off-season many fine players came there, including Moses Malone, then one of the top centers in the NBA. Hakeem learned from him, as well as from other NBA and former NBA players.

The coaches at Houston also worked with him. He had a lot of catching up to do. When practice for the 1981–1982 season began, Hakeem was finally a member of the team. He was now nearly 7 feet (213 centimeters) tall and weighed well over 200 pounds (91 kilograms).

The Cougars had a solid ball club that year. The stars were forwards Clyde Drexler and Larry Micheaux. Hakeem wasn't good enough to start at center, but he began to see action each game. That's when he learned he just wasn't fit enough to play for long periods of time.

Early in the season Hakeem often got back spasms. And if both teams ran the ball up and down for five minutes, Hakeem would find himself exhausted.

He finally started six games before the year ended. His scoring high was 20 points against Louisiana State University in December, and he had 8 blocks in a game against Texas Christian University in February. Coach Lewis said that shot blocking was Hakeem's best skill then.

The Cougars were not ranked in the top 20 at the end of the regular season. But they had a very solid 21–7 record and made it to the NCAA tournament. There they surprised everyone, making it to the fabled Final Four. Suddenly the team had a chance to win the national championship.

But in the semifinals, they faltered. Playing against North Carolina, a team with stars like James Worthy, Sam Perkins, and freshman Michael Jordan, the Cougars trailed all the way. Carolina came out fast and took a big 14–0 lead in the first few minutes. From his spot on the bench, Hakeem began to simmer.

"In that game he [Coach Lewis] didn't start me and they're [North Carolina] coming down the lane shooting layups," Hakeem said. "I was so mad. I was burning up."

It was 18-8 when Hakeem finally got into the action. He played 20 minutes, but had just 2 points and 6 rebounds. Houston lost the game 68–63 to finish their year at 25–8. The team would have most of their top players back next season—but would they have a good center?

In 1981–1982, Hakeem averaged just 8.3 points and 6.2 rebounds in 29 games. He also had 72 blocks and 25 dunks. Now, however, he had a burning desire to conquer this new game. But there was still no way to predict what kind of player he would become.

A STAR IS BORN

Hakeem knew he hadn't had a great year. Maybe he thought he should have played more, especially at the end of the season. But he did prove one thing: After playing the game for just three years, he was able to compete in Division I college basketball.

Hakeem's basketball skills improved rapidly. In his first season at Houston in 1981–1982, he wasn't a starter. But when he did get in, he quickly showed he was already an outstanding shot blocker.

Once again, he spent a great deal of time at the Fonde Recreation Center. "I played against a lot of pro players without knowing who they were," Hakeem said. "But because of that summer, I came back to Houston knowing I could play."

Four of the Houston starters in 1982–1983 looked very solid. Drexler and Micheaux were both potential All-Americans at forward. Michael Young and Alvin Franklin were good players at guard. If Hakeem did the job at center, the team could be one of the best.

It didn't take long to find out. The improvement in his game was almost incredible. His weight was up to about 240 pounds (109 kilograms), yet he was very quick underneath. His rebounding and shot-blocking skills were already superb. And his offense was improving by leaps and bounds.

There was no doubt in Coach Lewis's mind now: Hakeem was his starting center. And with the other outstanding players, the Houston Cougars were now a powerful and quick-striking team. As soon as the season started, they began rolling over opponents easily.

Led by Hakeem and Clyde Drexler, the Cougars loved to fast-break and finish by slam-dunking the ball home. That led to the team's getting the nickname "Phi Slamma Jamma." It was a play on the Greek letters used to name college fraternities. *Phi* was from the Greek alphabet. *Slamma Jamma* were made-up words and simply meant that they slammed and jammed the basketball.

As for Hakeem, he put together some outstanding games. He scored a career high of 30 points in a win over Utah. Against Southern Methodist Uni-

Hakeem was a much improved player in 1982–1983.
He soon became one of the leaders of a running, dunking
Houston attack that was dubbed Phi Slamma Jamma.

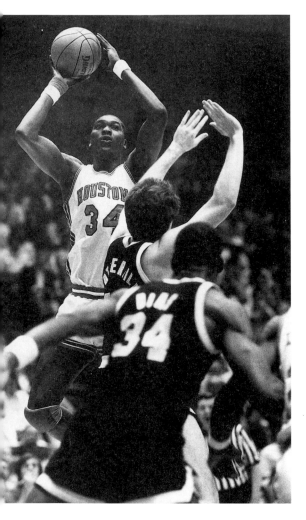

The top-ranked Cougars were a force throughout the 1982–1983 NCAA playoffs. Against Maryland, Hakeem shows he can shoot, too, as he cans a short jumper on the way to a Midwest Regional victory.

versity he had 22 rebounds. And he had 11 blocks against both Arkansas and Southwestern Louisiana, and 10 more against Texas. Opponents were hesitating about taking the ball to the hoop against the Cougars.

"He's got great foot movement," said Coach Lewis. "That's probably because of soccer. He can also run up and down the floor like a gazelle, and he's the best I've had since Elvin Hayes at moving laterally."

By the time the regular season ended, the entire country knew about Phi Slamma Jamma and Hakeem Olajuwon. Houston had a 27–2 record and was the number-one ranked team in the nation. Hakeem was being talked about as a bona fide All-American candidate. In one short year he had gone from a young, inexperienced center to a real star.

Next came the NCAA playoffs. The Cougars opened up by beating Maryland. Next they topped Memphis State as Hakeem scored 21 points. Against Villanova he was even better. He scored 20 points, hitting on 10 of 11 shots from the floor. He also had 13 rebounds and 8 big blocks. That victory put the Cougars into the Final Four once again.

In the semifinals they went up against a very good Louisville team. The Cardinals were in command right up to the midpoint of the second half. They held an 8-point lead when Houston and Hakeem suddenly took the game to another level. In the final part of the game, the big center simply took control on both ends of the court.

The Cougars wiped out the Louisville lead and came home with an easy 94–81 victory. Hakeem finished with 21 points, 22 rebounds, and 8 blocks. But with the game on the line in the second half he had 12 points, 15 rebounds, and 4 blocks.

Now the Cougars were in the final. They would be playing for the national championship against North Carolina State. N.C. State came into the tournament with just a 20–10 record. So Hakeem and the Cougars were big favorites.

From the beginning, North Carolina State slowed the pace so Houston couldn't run. They looked for good shots and were hitting them. At the half, the Wolfpack had a shocking 33–25 lead. But everyone knew what Phi Slamma Jamma had done to Louisville in the second half.

Sure enough, with Hakeem playing brilliantly, Houston opened the second half with a 15–2 run to go in front, 40–35. But then, with nine minutes left, Coach Lewis ordered his fast-breaking, running team to slow the pace. The strategy backfired. N.C. State kept it close, and with two minutes left they tied the score at 52 all.

Again Lewis ordered a stall, trying to play for the last shot. With a minute left, Alvin Franklin was fouled but missed the free throw. Now N.C. State had a chance to win it with 44 seconds remaining. They held the ball until there were just a few seconds left. Then Dereck Whittenburg tried an off-balance shot from way out front. Hakeem took a step toward the shooter, then whirled to wait for the rebound.

But the ball didn't even reach the rim. Suddenly, Wolfpack forward Lorenzo Charles cut in behind Hakeem, jumped, caught the air ball, and slammed it through the hoop at the buzzer. N.C. State had won, 54–52, to become the national champions.

It was a devastating loss for Hakeem and the Cougars. The big center had again been outstanding, with 20 points, 18 rebounds, and 11 blocks. He had been so good that despite his team's loss, he was named the Most Valuable Player in the tournament. In the five tourney games he averaged 18.8 points, 13 rebounds, and 6.4 blocked shots. But that didn't make losing any easier.

"When I think about that game I try not to think about the last minute," he would say. "I feel too bad just mentioning it. I know I don't want to be in that position again or feel like that again. It was heartbreaking."

In 34 games during his sophomore year, Hakeem had averaged 13.9 points and 11.4 rebounds, and had blocked 175 shots, for an average of 5.1 per game. He still didn't make a lot of All-American teams. Patrick Ewing of Georgetown and Ralph Sampson of Virginia were considered the top centers in college ball. But many of those who had played against Hakeem disagreed. To them, he was already the best.

In the NCAA championship game against North Carolina State, Hakeem scored 20 points, grabbed 18 rebounds, and blocked 11 shots. But the Cougars lost at the buzzer, 54–52.

ALL-AMERICAN SUPERSTAR

Even though he had an excellent year, Hakeem wasn't about to rest. He was studying business technology and had a 2.5 grade-point average, better than many student-athletes. And he still wanted to be a stronger basketball player.

That summer he played endlessly at the Fonde. His weight was up to 250 pounds (91 kilograms), and for the first time in three years Moses Malone didn't push him around. Hakeem acknowledged that he had made up his mind to play Malone tougher.

"This summer was different," he said. "The last two years Moses was just pushing me around using his body. This summer, I fought back. I decided I can't just be looking up to him all the time."

As soon as the 1983–1984 season began, it was easy to see that no one could really stop Hakeem. He had become a college superstar. With both Drexler and Larry Micheaux gone, Hakeem had to carry more of the load up front. And he was equal to the task.

Now the big games were the norm. On December 3, he made headlines by blocking 16 shots in a victory over Biscayne. A short time later he showed his improved offensive skills by scoring 35 against the University of California, Santa Barbara. Then in January he pulled down 25 rebounds as the Cougars walloped Texas Tech. He was doing it all.

Offensively, he was now shooting his short and medium jump shots with more confidence. He had also developed an impressive jump hook shot. His first step was as quick as that of a guard. And his spin moves around the

Hakeem improved his game by practicing at the Fonde Recreation Center in Houston during the summers. There he played often against NBA star center Moses Malone (left). Here the two meet as pros during Hakeem's rookie year with the Houston Rockets.

hoop left slower centers reaching for air. Yet scoring wasn't the first thing on his mind.

"I want to lead the nation in blocked shots and rebounds," Hakeem said. "I don't care about scoring, just as long as we win."

As the season continued, the praise poured in.

"The average big man doesn't get off the floor like Hakeem," said Kentucky center Sam Bowie, himself a 7-footer (213 centimeters tall). "He jumps with the spring of a man 6 feet 2 or 6 feet 3. Whenever I put the ball on the floor I say to myself, 'I wonder where Hakeem's coming from this time.' He is like six people out there."

Even his own coach, Guy Lewis, who had ridden Hakeem so hard his first two years, was surprised at the kind of player he had become.

"I never dreamed he would be this good," said Lewis. "When he first came here he couldn't make a layup. Now he has amazing timing. He's the greatest shot blocker I've ever seen."

When the regular season ended, the Cougars had a 28–4 record and were ranked number five in the nation. Their goal was still the national championship.

Once the NCAA playoffs began, Houston began rolling. First they topped Louisiana Tech, 77-69, then Memphis State, 78–71, and finally Wake Forest, 68-63. That gave them the Midwest Regional title and yet another trip to the Final Four. Against Wake Forest, Hakeem was super. He had 29 points on 14 of 16 shooting from the field.

In the NCAA semifinals, the Cougars whipped Virginia in overtime, 49-47. The team advanced to the championship game for a second straight year.

This time they would be meeting the Georgetown Hoyas. Georgetown was led by their own 7-foot (213-centimeter) All-American, Patrick Ewing.

The game was billed as a battle of the two best centers in college basketball. Unfortunately, it didn't turn out that way. Neither big man put on a great performance.

Hakeem was hampered by fouls, so he had to spend a good deal of time on the bench. Georgetown had the speed to run with the Cougars, and their swarming defense also hampered the Houston shooters. Basically, Ewing and Olajuwon played each other to a standoff.

Georgetown had a 40–30 lead at the half and basically maintained it to the end. The final was 84–75. The Hoyas were national champs, and Houston went home a loser again. Hakeem had just 15 points and 9 rebounds in the final game, while Ewing scored 10 and also had 9 rebounds.

But the entire year was a different story. Hakeem had a 16.8 scoring average in 37 games. He also led the nation with

As an all-American in 1983–1984, Hakeem led the Cougars back to the NCAA championship game. There he met another great center, Patrick Ewing (with ball), and the Georgetown Hoyas. The two big men played each other to a standoff, but Georgetown won the game, 84–75.

500 rebounds—a 13.5 average—and in blocked shots with 207—an average of 5.6 a game. By doing that, he had reached his preseason goals. Needless to say, he was a consensus All-American.

Hakeem had now been at Houston for four years. Because he had been red-shirted as a freshman, he could play basketball for another year. But the more he thought about it, the more he felt that it was time to move on. He soon announced he would leave Houston and enter the National Basketball Association draft.

ROCKETS SENSATION

There was little doubt that Hakeem was ready for the NBA. In fact, many people thought he would quickly become a superstar even though he had been playing basketball for only five years. That, in itself, was incredible.

The Houston Rockets had the first choice in the 1984 NBA draft. The year before, the Rockets drafted 7-foot 4-inch (224-centimeter) center Ralph Sampson of Virginia. But the team still had a poor 29–53 record. Would they draft another center?

Sure enough, the Rockets used their first pick to take Hakeem. That made him the top choice of the entire league. He signed a six-year contract worth some $6.3 million. Now he had to go out and prove himself all over again.

He soon had a new nickname, "Hakeem the Dream," and showed immediately that he could play in the NBA. But where would he play? Ralph Sampson had always been a center and was a good 4 inches (10 centimeters) taller than Hakeem. Yet it was easy to see that Hakeem was a stronger inside player than Sampson. So before the season began, it was decided that Sampson would play power forward with Hakeem as the starting center.

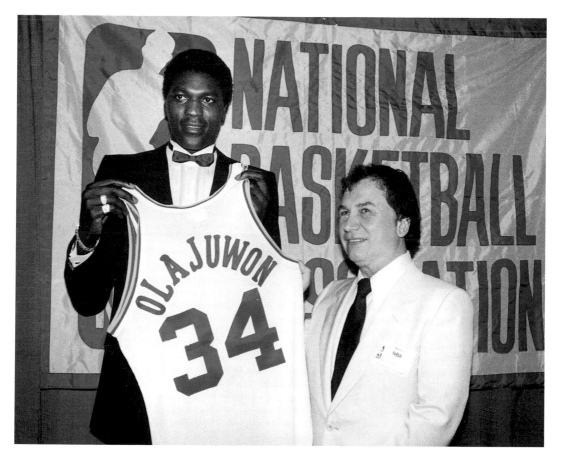

Hakeem decided to become a professional in 1984-1985 and was the first choice in the NBA draft. He was overjoyed to learn he would be staying in Houston when the Houston Rockets signed him to a $6.3 million contract. Here he shows off his Rockets jersey as team owner Charlie Thomas looks on.

In the first game of the 1984–1985 season, the Rockets looked good in topping the Dallas Mavericks, 121–111. Hakeem got off to a slow start, but in the second half he was tremendous. He scored 22 of his 24 points in that half. He also grabbed 9 rebounds. Sampson finished with 19 points and 13 rebounds. The two big men worked very well together.

The Rockets continued to play well, and Hakeem was making an impact immediately. He and Sampson were dubbed the "Twin Towers" by the press. Not too many players wanted to take it to the hoop against them.

Hakeem was having a great rookie year. When it ended, the Rockets had become winners, with a 48–34 record. They were second in the Midwest Division and had a 19-game improvement over the year before.

Hakeem finished the regular season with a 20.6 scoring average and an 11.9 per game rebounding mark. He also blocked 220 shots. Sampson led the team in scoring with a 22.1 average, grabbed 10.4 rebounds per game, and blocked 168 shots. Unfortunately, the team was eliminated in the first round of the playoffs by the Utah Jazz, 3 games to 2.

A short time later, Hakeem finished second in the Rookie of the Year voting to Michael Jordan of the Chicago Bulls. That was no disgrace. Jordan had also had a sensational first year.

In 1985–1986, Hakeem began to play like a real superstar and the Rockets almost won the NBA title. The team finished with a 51–31 record to win the Midwest Division. Hakeem led them in scoring with a 23.5 mark. He also averaged 11.5 rebounds and blocked 231 shots.

In the first round of the playoffs the Rockets swept the Sacramento Kings in three games. Then they topped the Denver Nuggets in six. Against Denver, Hakeem had games of 38, 31, 36, and 28 points. There were times when he seemed almost unstoppable.

Next came the L.A. Lakers, led by superstars Magic Johnson and Kareem Abdul-Jabbar. The Rockets took the Lakers out in just five games. Hakeem

When Hakeem joined the Rockets, Ralph Sampson moved from center to forward. The two big men were nicknamed the "Twin Towers" and played very well together.

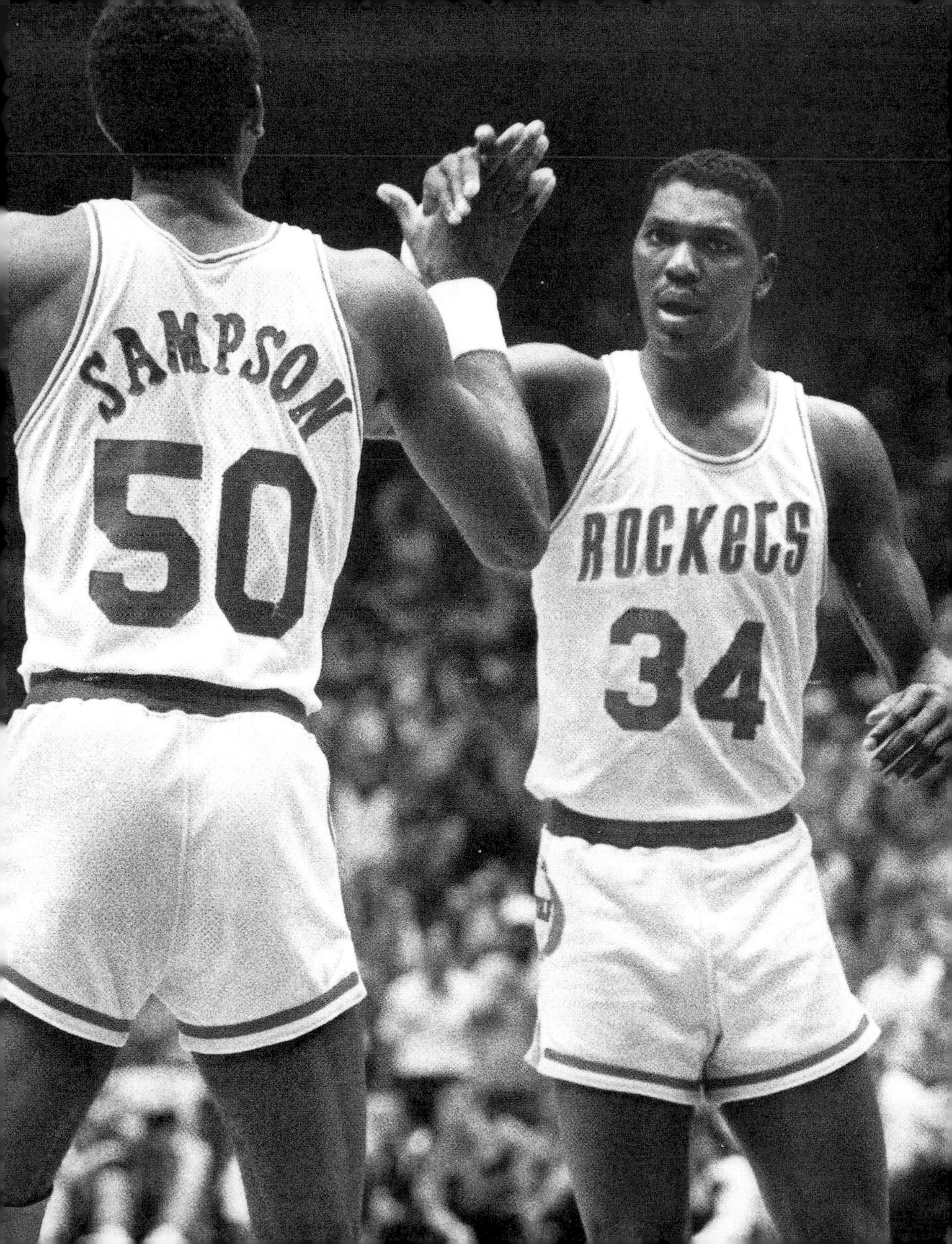
SAMPSON
50
ROCKETS
34

led his team in scoring in four of them with 28, 40, 35 and 30 points. He was having a tremendous playoff series. And now the Rockets were in the finals against Larry Bird and the Boston Celtics.

Boston proved too experienced for the Rockets. The Celts won the NBA championship in six games. Yet Hakeem had earned respect from the entire league. In 20 playoff games he averaged 26.9 points and 11.8 boards. After just two years in the league, he was an All-NBA second team choice and already considered one of the best.

BUILDING TOWARD A TITLE

Just when it looked as if the Rockets were becoming one of the NBA's better teams, things began going sour. In 1986–1987, Ralph Sampson was limited to 43 games because of injuries. Hakeem played well again, but the team finished with just a 42–40 record.

In the playoffs, the Rockets lost to Seattle in the second round. The game in which they were eliminated went into double overtime. Even though the Supersonics won, Hakeem turned a lot of heads when he scored a career-high 49 points. After the year ended he was named to the All-NBA first team for the first time.

Then in December of the 1987–1988 season, Ralph Sampson was traded to Golden State for center Joe Barry Carroll and guard Eric "Sleepy" Floyd. The Twin Towers were no more. Hakeem the Dream had become *the* big man on the Rockets. After the trade, the team finished with a winning record. Hakeem was All-NBA again, but the team was having a hard time getting through the first round of the playoffs.

In 1988–1989, Hakeem had his best season yet. He averaged 24.8 points a game, which was tenth best in the league. In fact, he was the only center in

the top ten. He also led the league in rebounding with a 13.5 mark, and was fourth
in blocked shots with 3.44 a game. In ad-
dition, he was sixth in the league in steals
with 2.60 per game.

After the season he was named to the
All-NBA first team for the third straight
year. But Hakeem didn't like the makeup
of the Rockets and said so. In his eyes, there
were too many selfish players who weren't
always trying hard enough.

Hakeem appeared to be right. The
team was just 41–41 in 1989–1990, even
though Olajuwon led the league in both
rebounding and blocked shots. Then the
next year the team appeared mediocre
again. They were just 16–13 on January 3,
1991, when they went up against the Chicago Bulls. Hakeem was going head-to-
head with Chicago center Bill Cartwright.

During a scramble underneath, Cartwright whirled around and his elbow
caught Hakeem flush in the face. It was an

*Hakeem and former college teammate Clyde
Drexler (right) had a happy reunion as teammates
during the 1989 NBA All-Star Game. Drexler was
a superstar with the Portland Trailblazers but had
remained close friends with Hakeem.*

accidental blow, but it fractured Hakeem's right orbit—the bone that houses the eye. He needed surgery right away and couldn't play for almost two months. With Hakeem out, everyone thought the team would fall apart. But they didn't.

It was as if all the other Rockets suddenly decided to play basketball again. They had depended too much on Hakeem. The team lost 7 of 10 after Hakeem was hurt, but then reversed itself and won 12 of the next 15.

Even Hakeem couldn't believe what he was seeing. "Guys diving for the ball, hungry guys," he said. "It was like, 'Look at me.' They finally had a chance to show what they could do."

Hakeem returned on February 28 and quickly found that the new Rockets style was also good for him.

"Ever since I came into this league I've been double-teamed," he explained. "But now that the offense is spread out, the game is suddenly easy. It's like in college. It's fun. When the game is over now, I'm not even tired. I could play another game."

At the end of the season the Rockets surprised everyone with a 52–30 record, third best in the Midwest Division. Even though they again lost early in the playoffs, it seemed like a turnaround year.

But then the club faltered again, slipping to 42–40 in 1991–1992. This time they missed the playoffs completely. There had also been a coaching change shortly after midseason. Former Rockets star Rudy Tomjanovich took over behind the bench. Everyone looked to a fresh start in 1992–1993.

An eye injury in 1991 kept Hakeem out of the lineup for almost two months. When he returned, it was with a different look—a pair of goggles to protect the injured eye. But nothing stopped him from playing his usual strong game.

Rookie forward Robert Horry joined the ball club that year, teaming with Otis Thorpe up front. Kenny Smith and Vernon Maxwell were a solid backcourt combo. There were also some new role players to come off the bench. And Hakeem still reigned in the middle.

The Houston team began to play very well. Hakeem was having a tremendous season. Just after the midpoint mark, it was announced that he had signed a new contract. It was a four-year extension worth about $26 million—up to $30 million with incentives.

Everyone on the team felt he was worth the money. Houston reserve guard Scott Brooks put it this way: "Night in and night out, Dream just picks us up and carries us."

At one point in the season the Rockets tied a franchise record by winning 13 games in a row. Hakeem was being talked about as a possible MVP. He had more offensive

Pure grace in the air, Hakeem floats with the ball.

moves than any other center and was scoring at a better clip than at any time in his career.

"I see my game as something creative, maybe something new," he said. "More moves, more fakes, more of the unexpected. I get great joy from losing my man completely."

The Rockets finished strong to win the Midwest Division with a 55–27 record. Only three teams had a better mark. Hakeem was fourth in scoring with a career best 26.1 average, was fourth in rebounds with 13.0 a game, and the leader in blocks with 342 for a 4.17 average. He was on the All-NBA first team and the All-Defensive team.

But there was a big disappointment in store. The Rockets were again eliminated from the playoffs. This time they were beaten in the conference semifinals by Utah, 4 games to 3.

For Hakeem and his teammates, there was still one more mountain to climb.

A YEAR OF AWARDS

The Rockets opened the 1993–1994 season like a team on a mission. Rookie guard Sam Cassell and third-year forward Carl Herrera gave the team added strength off the bench. And when the team won their first 15 games, they showed the rest of the league they meant business.

While everyone was playing well, it was Hakeem who had raised his already superior game to still another level. He was doing it in a year that would see him turn 31 before it ended. That isn't young for a basketball player, who has to run up and down the court during the long season. Yet he was playing with intensity at both ends, and the Rockets continued to win.

It was no surprise when the team won the Midwest Division a second straight year. This time they had set a franchise record with a 58–24 mark. Only Seattle in the Pacific Division had a better regular-season mark. And Hakeem had finished a very special season for him.

He had a career best 27.3 scoring average, third best in the league. He was fourth in rebounding with 11.9 per game and second in blocks with a 3.71 average. But it wasn't only the numbers. He had done everything a center could do. It was no surprise the awards starting coming.

First, he was named NBA Defensive Player of the Year for the second time in a row. And soon after the playoffs began, he was named the NBA's Most Valuable Player.

"After a while, I gave up thinking about winning the MVP," Hakeem admitted. "I just had fun trying to win a championship. That's my real goal, to win a championship."

In the eyes of everyone else, Hakeem was the right choice. Charles Barkley, of the Phoenix Suns, who had beaten out Hakeem for the MVP a year earlier, said it was no contest this time. "Hakeem is the MVP, period," Barkley said. "He's been the best player in the league this year."

But what Hakeem wanted to do most was lead his team to the title. The Rockets started their run by beating the Portland Trail Blazers in four games. Next came Barkley and the high-scoring Suns. It was a tough series that finally came down to a seventh and deciding game. Once again it was Hakeem who rose to the occasion. He scored 37 points and grabbed 17 rebounds as the Rockets won it, 104–94.

Hakeem was better than ever in 1993–1994. He was doing the job at both ends of the court as the Rockets got off to a 15–0 start. In the eyes of most, he was the best player in the league, playing hard every night, as he shows here in a game against the tough Phoenix Suns.

Then it was on to the conference finals against the Utah Jazz. This time the
Rockets weren't about to falter. They
whipped the Jazz in just five games and
were in the NBA finals. Now the Rockets had to meet Patrick Ewing and the
New York Knicks. It promised to be an
epic battle.

It turned out to be a rough, physical
series. The Knicks were the best defensive team in the league. Ewing, Charles
Oakley, Anthony Mason, Derek Harper,
and John Starks would wear their opponents down. Because of the tight style of
play, each game was close and came down
to the final minutes.

The clubs split the first two games at
Houston. The Rockets won the first, 85–
78, and the Knicks the second, 91–83. In
game three, a double-teamed Olajuwon
threw an outlet pass to rookie Cassell, who
hit a 3-pointer in the final seconds to win

*When the Rockets met the New York Knicks in
the NBA finals, Hakeem went against his old
college foe, Patrick Ewing (right), once again.
Here the two battle for a rebound. Hakeem is
clearly in a better position to go after the ball.*

the game. But then the Knicks won the next two to give them a 3–2 lead and put them a game away from the title. Hakeem would need a big effort in game six to keep the Rockets in the hunt.

That was the game in which he blocked Starks's 3-point try at the buzzer to preserve an 86–84 win for the Rockets. Now it came down to one game for the championship. Hakeem wanted that more than anything else.

"A championship is team glory," he said, "where the MVP is an individual honor. You always have to take the team first."

Like the first six games, this one was very close. Neither the Rockets nor the Knicks could break it open. The Knicks fought and scrapped, but their guards weren't shooting well. At the same time, Houston's guards (Smith, Maxwell, and Cassell) were on their game. But the big difference was in the middle. Hakeem was once again outplaying Patrick Ewing, scoring on a variety of dunks, jumpers, and hooks. And when he didn't have the shot, he was spotting open teammates.

When it ended, the Rockets had a 90–84 victory and, better yet, the NBA championship. The players and fans went wild. It was a celebration that was a long time coming. And no one was happier than Hakeem Olajuwon. This was the one thing he had never done in basketball — helped his team win a title.

In the final game he had 25 points, 10 rebounds, and 7 assists. It came as no surprise when he was named the Most Valuable Player in the finals. Yet he watched the celebration rather quietly.

There was little doubt that Hakeem outplayed Ewing for most of the championship series. He was just quicker, rebounded, and shot better.

"In the locker room I just sat back and reflected," Hakeem said. "I saw everybody celebrating. That was something you picture in your mind before. But I actually enjoyed that moment of peace, just watching everyone celebrating."

Houston guard Kenny Smith said more: "With one game for the championship, you have to think that the best player on your team is going to carry you to the title. We *knew* Hakeem would do it for us."

Hakeem Olajuwon has emerged as a man at peace. He has stayed close to his large family. Three of his brothers live near him in Houston, while one brother and sister live in Nigeria. Hakeem's parents visit the United States whenever they can (they were in Houston to watch the Rockets win the NBA championship in 1994).

Hakeem holds his trophy for Most Valuable Player in the finals, as the Rockets celebrate the NBA Championship. A few weeks earlier he had been named the Most Valuable Player for the entire season.

Even as a top NBA star, Hakeem loves to visit kids at schools and hospitals. He has never forgotten his childhood in Nigeria and knows how lucky he was to come to Houston and become a basketball great. Now he wants to help other youngsters find their way.

Hakeem has worked for various charities. He has been the honorary chairman for a UNICEF benefit for Rwandan children and has volunteered for the Make-A-Wish Foundation.

The Islamic religion remains very important to Hakeem. He prays every day and refuses to eat red meat. But the competitive fires within him still burn. Otherwise, he couldn't have produced the greatest season of his life at the age of 31.

When he looked back at his team's march to the championship, Hakeem thought of how many times the Rockets had to come back. That's what he thought was so great about the whole thing.

"You have to enjoy the journey," he said, "not just the destination."

Hakeem might have been talking about his entire life. The destination was basketball stardom. But the journey to get there—from Lagos, Nigeria, to Houston, Texas—was the most amazing thing of all.

53 9:06
ROCKETS
PLYR FOULS PNTS
45
PLYR FOULS PNTS.
3 13 4
FULL TIME OUTS :20
5
PERIOD
1
FULL TIME OUTS :20
TEAM FOULS
Panasonic.
5
1
TEAM FOULS
1
Enjoy Coca-Cola
Genuine Draft
L.A. SPORTS ARENA
HOUSTON
34
Clippers
ROCKETS

HAKEEM OLAJUWON: HIGHLIGHTS

1963   Born on January 21 in Lagos, Nigeria.

1980   Arrives at the University of Houston.

1982   Becomes Houston Cougars' starting center for 1982–1983 season.

1983   University of Houston reaches tournament finals.
        Named MVP of NCAA tournament.

1984   Named All-American and College Player of the Year. Again leads University
        of Houston to NCAA finals.
        Taken first in the NBA draft, by Houston Rockets.

1985   Makes NBA All-Rookie first team.

1986   Leads Rockets to NBA finals. Named to All-NBA second team.

1987   Named to All-NBA first team and All-NBA defensive first team.

1988   Again named to All-NBA first team and All-NBA defensive first team.

1989   Again named to All-NBA first team. Becomes first player to record 200 steals
        and 200 blocked shots in a single season.

1990   Named to All-NBA second team and All-NBA defensive first team.

1991   Misses 25 straight games because of eye injury.
        Named to All-NBA third team and All-NBA defensive second team.

1992   Selected to play in seventh straight NBA All-Star Game, a Houston Rockets
        record.

1993   Named NBA Defensive Player of the Year.
        Named to All-NBA first team and All-NBA defensive first team.

1994   Leads Rockets to NBA title.
        Becomes first player in history to be named NBA regular-season MVP, NBA
        finals MVP, and Defensive Player of the Year in the same season.

1995   Rockets win second consecutive NBA championship; Olajuwon
        named finals MVP.

FIND OUT MORE

Aaseng, Nathan. *Basketball's Playmakers*. Minneapolis: Lerner, 1983.

Anderson, Dave. *The Story of Basketball*. New York: Morrow Junior Books, 1988.

Basketball: *Superstars & Superstats*. Racine, Wis.: Western Publishing, 1991.

Gutman, Bill. *Basketball*. North Bellmore, N.Y.: Marshall Cavendish, 1990.

Rekela, George R. *Hakeem Olajuwon: Tower of Power*. Minneapolis: Lerner, 1993.

Slam-Dunk Champions. Racine, Wis.: Western Publishing, 1993.

How to write to Hakeem Olajuwon:

Hakeem Olajuwon
c/o Houston Rockets
The Summit
Ten Greenway Plaza
Houston, TX 77046

INDEX